Plastic

Andrew Langley

WAYLAND

First published in 2008
by Wayland

Wayland
338 Euston Road
London NW1 3BH

Wayland Australia
Level 17/207 Kent Street
Sydney, NSW 2000

Editor: Annabel Savery
Designer: Ian Winton
Illustrator: Ian Winton
Picture researcher: Rachel Tisdale

Acknowledgements: Corbis: cover (Perry Mastrovito), 12 (David Rubinger). Getty Images: 6 (Henry Georgi), 11 (Peter Ginter), 18 (Jeff Marmelstein). Istockphoto: cover and spread head panel (Charles Benavidez), title page and 21 (Jan Vancura), 5 (Aleksandr Lobanov), 7 (Leslie Banks), 9 (Asier Villafranca Velasco), 14 inset (Joe Gough), 15 (Floria Marius Catalin), 17 (Jane Pang), 19 (René Mansi), 20 (Frank van Haalen). The LEGO Group: 10, 13. NASA: 16. Richard Bowater: 4. Science Photo Library: 8 (Paul Rapson), 14 main (Peter Ryan).

British Library Cataloguing in Publication Data
Langley, Andrew
    Plastic. - (Everyday materials)
    1. Plastics - Juvenile literature
    I. Title
    620.1'923

ISBN–13: 978 0 75025 318 5

Printed in China

Wayland is a division of Hachette Children's Books,
an Hachette Livre UK company.

Contents

What is plastic?

Plastic is a **synthetic material**. This is not a natural material but one that has been made by people.

The fabric for hot-air balloons is made from a type of plastic.

Plastic can be made into any kind of shape. It can be any colour, or it can be clear like glass.

Eye spy

Find three things made of plastic in your classroom.

All kinds of plastic

Plastic can be hard, like a button on a shirt. It can be very strong, like a bike helmet.

In a sponge plastic is soft. In a garden hose it is bendy. In a toy it can be squeezy.

What is plastic made of?

Most plastic is made from **oil**. Oil is a **raw material**. Plastic can also be made from other raw materials such as wood and cotton.

Plastic is very cheap to produce. So things made from plastic are often cheap for us to buy.

Plastic windmills

What do you think?

Which costs the most money – a gold ring or a plastic ring?

Resin into plastic

Plastic is made in two parts. First, the raw material is mixed with gas and chemicals. These turn it into a mixture called **resin**. This resin is made into **granules**.

Resin granules

In the second part, the resin granules are heated and become liquid. Now the liquid resin can be made into a shape.

Did you know?

Plastic makers add special chemicals to the liquid resin to give it colour.

Moulding and casting

Plastic can be shaped by moulding or **casting**. In moulding, a machine presses the hot, liquid resin into a **mould**. The resin goes hard as it cools down.

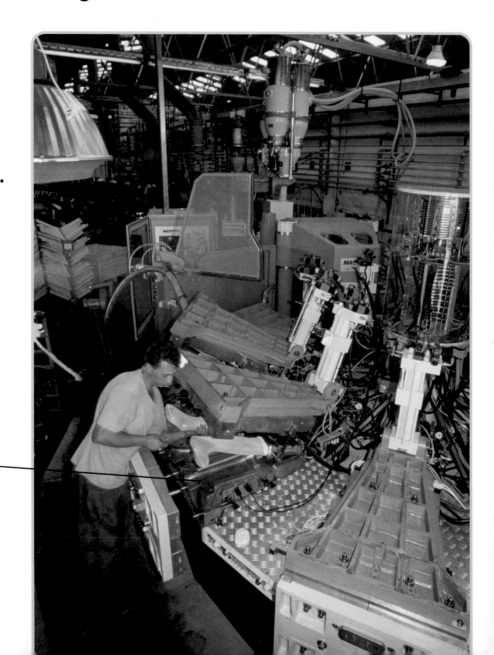

This mould is used to make plastic boots.

These plastic bricks have been shaped and hardened inside the machine.

In casting, the hot, liquid resin is poured into a mould. Chemicals help the plastic to harden.

Eye spy

If you blow into a balloon, it will fill up with air. In the same way, a machine blows air into plastic to make bottles.

Extruding and laminating

An **extruding** machine squeezes hot resin through a small hole. The plastic comes out in a long, thin stream. It has the same shape as the hole. Extruding machines make hoses and pipes.

Plastic pipes

Eye spy

Think of squeezing toothpaste out of a tube. That is how an extruding machine works.

Plastic is often used in **laminating**. Layers of plastic can be squashed together with other materials to make them stronger.

Layers of laminated wood

Special uses

We use plastic in all kinds of special ways.
Scientists plan to make **space satellites**
out of laminated plastic and metal.

Space satellite

Plastic contact lens

In hospitals, doctors fix broken bones with plastic screws. Plastic **lenses** help people to see better.

Eye spy

Look at the labels on your clothes. Do they say **nylon** or **polyester**? These are kinds of plastic.

Recycling plastic

People throw away millions of plastic things every day. Plastic does not **rot** away quickly, like paper or wood.

Now we can use plastic again. It can be cut up and melted. Then it can be turned into a new plastic object.

What do you think?

One day, we will have used up all the Earth's oil. What can we use instead of plastic?

Quiz

Questions

1. What is most plastic made of?
2. What happens when plastic resin granules are heated?
3. What kind of machine makes plastic pipes?
4. What do we call something made of layers of plastic and other materials?
5. What is polyester?

Answers

1. Most plastic is made of oil.
2. When resin granules are heated they melt.
3. An extruding machine makes plastic pipes.
4. It is called laminated material.
5. Polyester is a kind of plastic used for making clothes.

Plastic topic web

Geography
The oil that plastic is made from comes from all over the world. Places like Nigeria in Africa have lots of oil.

Sports and PE
Lots of sports equipment is made from plastic. Even the bottoms of your trainers are made from a type of plastic.

History
Plastic was first used in 1869 to make billiard balls. Billiards is a game like snooker.

Art and design
You can make lots of things out of plastic. Look in shops for kits to make model boats and planes.

Science
The oil that is used to make plastic comes from under the ground. It takes thousands of years to form from dead animals and plants.

Glossary

casting pouring a liquid into a mould; when it goes hard it will have the shape of the mould

extruding squeezing melted plastic resin through a special hole

granules small pieces of a material

laminating squashing together layers of plastic and other materials

lenses specially shaped pieces of plastic (or glass) which make things look bigger or clearer

mould a shaped container, when liquid is put in; it will fill the shape of the mould

nylon a kind of plastic used to make cloth or thread

oil a natural material which comes from under the ground, people use it as fuel; or to make other materials such as plastic

polyester a kind of plastic used to make cloth or thread

raw material a natural material that is found in the earth; it can be used to make other products

resin a material made from oil; this is the first stage of making plastic

rot to waste away and disappear

space satellite a small craft which goes round the Earth in space, satellites are used to send TV and radio signals; and to help track the world's weather

synthetic material a material which is not natural; but made by people

Further information

Books to read

Find Out About: Find Out About Plastic. Henry Pluckrose.
   Franklin Watts Ltd, 2002.

Our World: Plastics. Katie Jackson Bedford. Franklin Watts Ltd, 2005.

Raintree Perspectives: Using Materials: How We Use Plastic. Chris Oxlade.
   Raintree Publishers, 2004.

Reduce, Reuse, Recycle: Plastic. Alexandra Fix. Heinemann, 2007.

Start-Up Science: Materials. Claire Llewellyn. Evans Brothers Ltd, 2004.

Web sites to visit

BBC Schools
http://www.bbc.co.uk/schools/scienceclips/ages/5_6/sorting_using_mate.shtml
Learn all about different types of materials and their properties.

http://www.recycling-guide.org.uk/plastic.html
Learn all about how to recycle plastic.

http://www.olliesworld.com/uk/html/sortgame.html
Ollie Recycles is a website for kids all about the 3Rs – 'Reduce, Re-use, Recycle.'

Index